ANGRY BIRDS™
PIGS ON BIRD ISLAND

Popcorn
ELT
Readers

eggs

There are three **eggs**.

fly

They can **fly**.

explode

It **explodes**.

island

They live on an **island**.

pig

This is a **pig**.

ship

This is a **ship**.

play music

They like to **play music**.

worried

The man is **worried**.

Where's the popcorn?
Look in your book.
Can you find it?

Meet the birds

This is Bird **Island**. The birds here can't **fly**. They have a lot of **eggs**.

This is Red. He is always angry. He goes to a class for angry birds.

Matilda is the teacher. She has four angry birds in her class: Red, Chuck, Bomb and Terence.

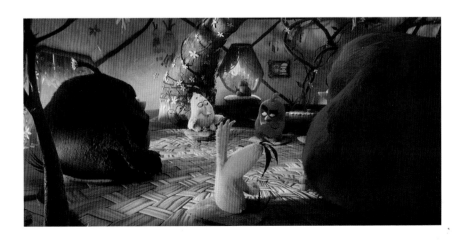

Chuck is a small bird. He talks quickly and he walks quickly.

Bomb is a big, black bird. Sometimes he **explodes**.

Terence is a very big bird, but he is quiet.
He does not talk.

Piggy **Island** is not far from Bird **Island**. The **pigs** here are green. They live in a big town.

The **pigs** like to dance and **play music**.

The **pigs** like to sleep and eat. They are always hungry.

Leonard is a big **pig** and he is very bad.
He wants **eggs** for dinner.

One day the birds see a **ship** on the sea. The **ship** comes to their **island**.

Some green **pigs** come from the **ship**.
They dance and play for the birds.

The birds are happy. They dance too.

Red goes home. He is not happy.

In the morning, Red sees a second **ship**.
There are more **pigs** on the **ship**.

There are a lot of **pigs** on Bird **Island** now.

Red is **worried**. What do the pigs want?
What do you think?

THE END

After you read

1 Match the pictures with the sentences.

i) He explodes.	b
ii) She is a teacher.	☐
iii) He walks very quickly.	☐
iv) He is a small green pig.	☐
v) They are happy.	☐

2 Look at the pictures. Choose the correct word.

go   talk   dance   wants   ~~fly~~

a) The birds cannot <u>f</u> <u>l</u> <u>y</u> .

b) Terence does not _ _ _ _ .

c) The pigs _ _ _ _ _ _ .

d) They _ _ to a class for angry birds.

e) Leonard _ _ _ _ _ eggs for dinner.

3 Find the words in the eggs.

quiet ~~angry~~ happy quick worried

a) <u>a</u> <u>n</u> g <u>r</u> <u>y</u> .

b) <u>q</u> _ _ _ <u>t</u> .

c) <u>q</u> _ _ _ <u>k</u> .

d) <u>h</u> _ _ _ <u>y</u> .

e) <u>w</u> _ _ _ _ _ <u>d</u> .

4 Draw a bird. Write a sentence.

My bird is ....

Quiz time!

Answer the questions. Yes or No?

		Yes	No
1)	Red is happy.	☐	☐
2)	Chuck talks very quickly.	☐	☐
3)	Terence is very small.	☐	☐
4)	Leonard does not like eggs.	☐	☐
5)	The pigs play music.	☐	☐

SCORES

How many of your answers are correct?

0–2: Read the book again! Can you answer the questions now?

3–4: Good work! The birds like you!

5: Wow! Are you Red's friend?

1 🔘 **Listen and read.**

Pigs on Bird Island

Angry class for angry birds,
Red is angry,
Red is angry.

Chuck is quick, Bomb is big,
Red is angry,
Red is angry.

Leonard's green and he's a pig,
And he's hungry,
And he's hungry.

Leonard comes in a ship,
And he's hungry,
And he's hungry.

Hungry pigs,
Angry birds.
Hungry pigs,
ANGRY BIRDS!

2 🔘 **Say the chant.**